Animals
of the Bible

FOR YOUNG CHILDREN

Marie-Hélène Delval • Aurélia Fronty

Animals
of the Bible

FOR YOUNG CHILDREN

Eerdmans Books for Young Readers

Grand Rapids, Michigan ✤ Cambridge, U.K.

This selection of Bible stories, paraphrased for young readers, uses language and imagery appropriate for children while remaining faithful to the spirit of the biblical texts.

In the Beginning

When it all began,
the breath of God floated over the waters.
God made the earth, the sky,
the sea, and everything in them.
The sky surrounded the earth
and was reflected in the water.
Now life could be born!

Creatures of the Water

God said,
"Let the waters swarm with living things!"
And God created the great sea snakes,
the fish, and all the creatures
that slide and swim in the water.

Creatures of the Air

God said,
"Let birds fill the air!"
And God created the birds
flying in the sky
above the earth,
and all the creatures with wings.

Creatures of the Land

God said,
"Let the earth be filled with wild animals
and all kinds of creatures
that run and jump and crawl on the ground!"
God saw that it was beautiful.
Then God said,
"Let more and more and more animals
fill the water, the air, and the earth!"

Names for the Animals

God grew a great big garden,
and put Adam, a man, in it.
God brought all the animals to Adam
so that Adam could give them each a name:
cow, tiger, turtle, mosquito, and parrot;
hippopotamus and swallow, jellyfish and elephant,
wolf, lion, rabbit, eel, and antelope.
For each animal Adam met,
he invented a name.

The Lying Snake

The snake was sly and sneaky.
He said to Eve,
"Taste the fruit that God told you not to eat."
Eve ate the fruit and gave some to Adam.
Then they saw that they were not strong like God.
They were weak, and naked,
as naked as the snake!
And they were ashamed.

Abel's Lamb

Abel offered to God the lambs from his flock.
His brother Cain offered to God
some fruit of the earth
that he was proud to have grown.
God loved Abel's lamb,
but he wasn't interested in Cain's fruit.
Cain became angry and killed Abel.
Then God punished Cain by sending him away.

Soon there was so much fighting on the earth
that God wanted to destroy
everything he had made.
But God loved Noah. So God said to him,
"The rain will fall
for forty days and forty nights,
and everything will be covered with water.
Build an ark, a big boat.
Bring with you two of each kind of animal
that lives on the earth."

Noah's Raven

When the rain stopped
and the water began to dry up,
Noah sent out a raven.
And the raven flew away,
black against the black of the sky and the water.
At night, the raven came back,
because he could not find a place to land.

Noah's Dove

Noah waited seven more days,
and he sent out a dove.
The dove flew away,
and when she returned,
white against the morning sky,
she held in her beak
a small olive branch:
the earth was dry!

Noah and his family left the ark.
He let all the creatures go —
the beetles, crocodiles, and crabs,
hedgehogs, hyenas, and scorpions,
zebras, ladybugs, and all the others.
Before long, there would be thousands
of animals on the earth again.
And the beautiful rainbow from God
shone above them.

Abraham's Ram

Abraham wanted to please God.
He was ready to sacrifice Isaac, his son,
his only child, to God.
But the angel of God called to him,
"No! No! Don't hurt your boy!"
Then Abraham saw a ram
whose horns were caught in the bushes.
He offered the ram to God, and God promised him,
"You will have as many children
as there are stars in the sky!"

God's people were slaves in Egypt.
Pharaoh, the king of Egypt,
would not let them go.
God said to Moses,
"Stretch your stick over the marsh!"
Immediately, frogs jumped out by the thousands,
and they covered everything in Egypt.
What a plague!

Then God said to Moses,
"Hit the ground with your stick!"
And the dust of the ground turned into mosquitoes
that buzzed and bit the animals and the people.
But Pharaoh still said "No!"
Then came the flies.
The big flies were everywhere:
in houses, even in the king's palace.
What a plague!

The Grasshoppers

Then God made the wind blow,
and the wind brought grasshoppers.
There were so many grasshoppers
that no one could see the sun!
The grasshoppers ate everything:
wheat, vegetables, the leaves of trees.
What a plague!
Pharaoh was stubborn. He still said "No!"
But not for much longer . . .

The Bees of Canaan

Finally, Pharaoh let the Israelites go.
The people of God
walked in the desert,
and Moses showed them the way.
They went to the country that God gave them:
Canaan, the Promised Land,
the land flowing with milk and honey,
the sweet honey from the bees.

Balaam's Donkey

God was angry with Balaam
and sent an angel to block Balaam's path.
Three times, the donkey saw the angel and stopped.
Three times, Balaam beat his donkey.
Then God made the donkey talk. The donkey said,
"Why do you beat me, Master?
I have always carried you well!"
Then Balaam saw the angel too
and he bowed down
to listen to what God wanted to say.

Samson's Foxes

God made Samson very, very strong.
But in Samson's country
there were enemy soldiers everywhere.
Samson caught three hundred foxes.
He tied their tails together, two by two.
Then he put a torch between their tails
and let them run wild in the enemies' fields:
their wheat, their grapevines, and their olive trees
all burned to the ground.

The Deer

"As the deer who wants to drink
looks for water from the river,
My soul looks for God.
I am thirsty for God."

The Sparrow and the Swallow

"The sparrow has found a safe place,
and the swallow has found a nest for its babies.
Like them, I am safe in your house,
oh Lord, my God!"

The Sparrow and the Stork

"God, you have planted big trees.
In the cedars the sparrow builds its nest,
and the stork lives in the cypress tree."

The Hippopotamus

God said,
"Look at the hippopotamus!
I'm the one who made him!
He eats grass like an ox.
What a nice back! What a beautiful belly!
His legs are tough; his bones are strong.
Yes, he is a masterpiece!"

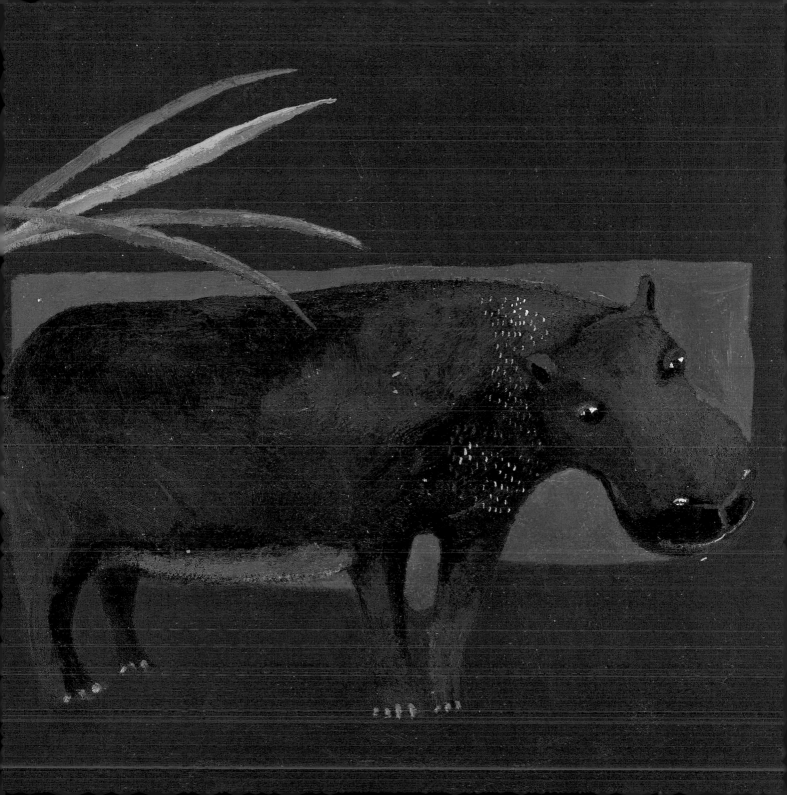

The Ants and the Lizards

There are some little creatures
that are very extraordinary.
All summer long, the tiny ants
store up food for the winter,
and the lizards walk around
at home in the king's palace!

The Cats of Babylon

There was a time when the people of God
were prisoners in Babylon.
Jeremiah the prophet
told them what the Lord said:
"Look at these idols made of wood, gold, and silver!
Don't be afraid, they are not gods;
cats walk right over them.
You worship the only true God."

Daniel's Lions

In Babylon, when Darius was king,
no one was allowed to pray to God.
But Daniel prayed in his room.
Someone told the king, and Daniel was punished;
he was thrown into the lion's den.
The next day, the king came to see:
Daniel was alive!
The lions did not hurt him!
And King Darius believed in Daniel's God.

Jonah's Fish

God was angry with Jonah.
He sent a big storm at sea.
Then Jonah said to the sailors,
"It's my fault! Throw me overboard!"
God sent a huge fish
to swallow Jonah.
For three days and three nights
Jonah prayed in the belly of the fish.
And the fish spit Jonah onto the shore.

The Cow and the Bear

Isaiah the prophet said,
"One day a child will be born.
God's spirit will be in him,
and he will bring peace:
the wolf will live with the lamb,
the cow and the bear will be friends,
and the baby will play with the cobra.
The love of God will fill the earth
just like the water fills the sea!"

The Sheep and the Shepherds

One night, on a hillside,
shepherds were watching their sheep.
An angel came to them,
surrounding them with the light of God.
The angel said to them,
"I bring you news of great joy:
today, a Savior is born.
He is a baby lying in a manger."

The Dove of Jesus

Jesus came to the edge of the Jordan River
to be baptized by John, a prophet of God.
When Jesus was baptized and came out of the water,
the Spirit of God came down in the form of a dove.
And the people heard a voice from heaven saying,
"Here is my son;
I love him with all my heart!"

An Egg or a Scorpion?

Jesus said to the people,
"Imagine a father who,
when his child asks for an egg,
would give him a scorpion!
God is the best of fathers.
Ask! He will give you
everything that is good for you."

The Demons and the Pigs

Jesus met a man possessed by demons
who wanted to hurt him.
Jesus said to the demons, "Get out of him!"
The demons begged,
"Then let us go into these pigs!"
Jesus let them go.
And the whole herd of pigs
threw themselves into the sea.
Then the man and his country were free
from the cruel demons.

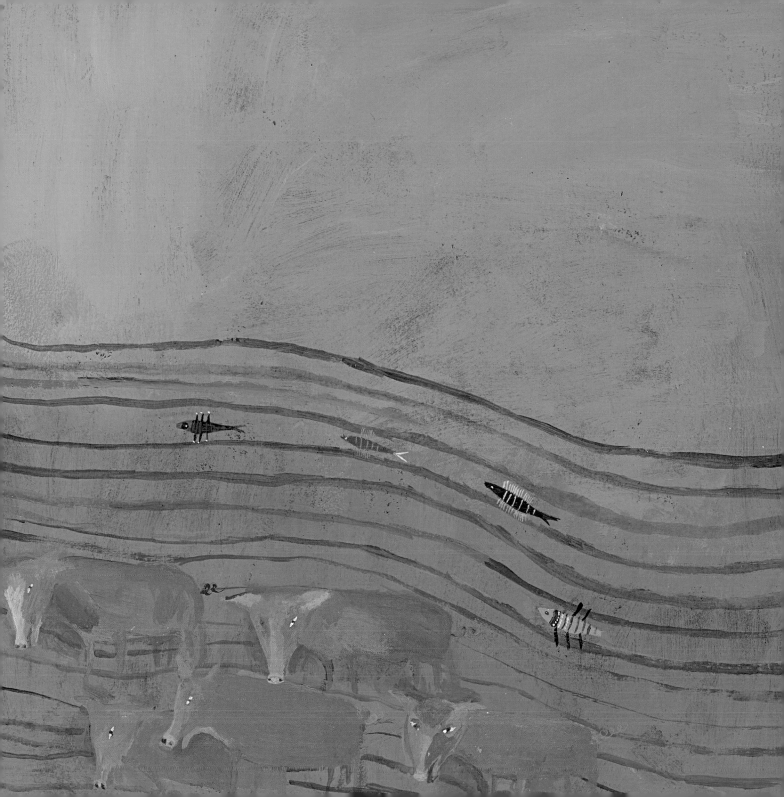

The Sparrows

Jesus said to the people,
"Don't be afraid!
You are all precious to God.
Look at the little sparrows:
God, your Father, takes care of them.
And you are more special to him
than all the sparrows in the sky!"

The Lost Sheep

Jesus told a story:
"A shepherd has one hundred sheep.
If he loses one,
he leaves all the others
to look for the one that is lost."
And Jesus said,
"God is like the shepherd.
He does not want to lose
any of his precious children!"

The Camel

Jesus said to his friends,
"The more money and things you have,
the harder it is to share
with those who have nothing.
I tell you, it is easier for a camel
to pass through the eye of a needle
than for a rich man
to enter the kingdom of God!"

Jesus and the Donkey

Jesus came to Jerusalem, the big city.
He rode on the back of a little donkey.
And the people called out joyfully,
"Blessed are you, who comes from God!"

The Hen and Her Chicks

Jesus looked at the city, and he was sad
because many people were angry with him
and wanted to kill him.
He said, "Jerusalem,
I have longed to protect your children
like a hen shelters her chicks under her wings.
But you did not want me to!"

Peter's Rooster

The soldiers had arrested Jesus.
Some people came to Peter and said,
"You — you are a friend of that Jesus!"
Peter was afraid. Three times he cried "No!"
Then a rooster crowed, and Peter remembered.
Jesus had said to him, "Before the rooster crows,
you will say three times
that you are not my friend!"
And Peter began to cry.

The Fish in the Lake

After Jesus had died,
Peter and his friends went fishing on the lake.
They worked all night for nothing.
In the morning, they saw a man on the shore.
He told them, "Cast your nets again!"
And this time, the nets were loaded with fish.
Then they understood:
the man on the shore was Jesus.
He was alive!

The Dragon

John, a friend of Jesus, had a dream.
He saw in the sky a fiery red dragon,
with seven heads and ten horns.
The archangel Michael and his angels
were fighting against him.
The dragon was defeated, and now
there is no place for him in heaven.
Then a voice proclaimed,
"This is the time of salvation!
This is the kingdom of God!"

All the Creatures

"How many are your works, oh Lord!
Your creatures fill the earth.
You open your hand and feed them;
you breathe your breath
and you give them life."

To find the full text of the stories retold in
Animals of the Bible for Young Children:

© 2005 Bayard Éditions Jeunesse as *Les Animaux de la Bible pour les petits*

This edition published in 2010 by
Eerdmans Books for Young Readers,
an imprint of William B. Eerdmans Publishing Co.
2140 Oak Industrial Dr. NE, Grand Rapids, Michigan 49505
P.O. Box 163, Cambridge CB3 9PU U.K.

www.eerdmans.com/youngreaders

Manufactured at Toppan Leefung Printing Ltd in Guangdong Province, China, February 2010, first printing

10 11 12 13 14 15 16 17   10 9 8 7 6 5 4 3 2 1

Library of Congress Cataloging-in-Publication Data

Delval, Marie-Hélène.
[Animaux de la Bible pour les petits. English.]
Animals of the Bible / by Marie-Hélène Delval ; illustrated by Aurélia Fronty.
p. cm.
Includes bibliographical references and index.
ISBN 978-0-8028-5376-9 (alk. paper)
1. Animals in the Bible — Juvenile literature. I. Title.
BS663.D4513 2010
220.8'59--dc22
2010005159

Other books in this series:

Psalms for Young Children
Marie-Hélène Delval • Arno

The Bible for Young Children
Marie-Hélène Delval • Götting